YEAR 9

T0363248

WRITING

NAPLAN*-FORMAT PRACTICE TESTS
with answers

Essential preparation for Year9
NAPLAN* Tests in WRITING

Alfred Fletcher

CORONEOS PUBLICATIONS

YEAR 9 WRITING
NAPLAN*- FORMAT PRACTICE TESTS with answers
© Alfred Fletcher 2010
Published by Coroneos Publications 2010

ISBN 978-1-921565-52-6

* These tests have been produced by Coroneos Publications independently of Australian governments and are not officially endorsed publications of the NAPLAN program

THIS BOOK IS AVAILABLE FROM RECOGNISED BOOKSELLERS OR CONTACT:

Coroneos Publications
Telephone: (02) 9624 3 977   Facsimile: (02) 9624 3717
Business Address: 6/195 Prospect Highway Seven Hills 2147
Postal Address: PO Box 2 Seven Hills 2147
Website: www. coroneos.com.au or www.basicskillsseries.com
E-mail: coroneospublications@westnet.com.au

Contents

NOTE:

- Students have 40 minutes to complete a test.

- Students must use 2B or HB pencils only.

Introductory Notes and the NAPLAN* Test

This book is designed to help you practise for the Writing section of the NAPLAN* test and develop the skills necessary to competently handle any writing task presented to you at this stage of your development. To date the NAPLAN* test has been only a narrative but here we have included examples of other types of writing you will experience during your schooling. Practicing these will develop skills that will assist you in all areas of your writing.

Also included in this book are some hints on how to improve your writing. Follow these hints and use them in your work as they may assist you in gaining additional vital marks under examination conditions. They will also help you develop your vocabulary which is vital to good, concise and clear writing.

We wish you all the best for the exam and know that the activities and tasks in this book will assist you in reaching your writing potential.

The Writing Task

The NAPLAN* test includes a writing task which has been narrative based. A narrative is basically a story that is in time order and is used to entertain and emotionally change an audience. The narrative form follows a common pattern of orientation [introduction], complication [problem] and resolution [conclusion]. A narrative can also inform, persuade and just be for social purposes.

With a narrative you have a great choice of what to write and as long as you follow the basic pattern you can be as creative as you like. This gives you, as a writer, the opportunity to show the full range of your abilities creatively but also use a wide range of vocabulary, show solid sentence structure and paragraphing and develop character and setting for a particular audience.

The test will give you a topic such as space, animals, work or family. It will also give you some stimulus material on a sheet which may be images [pictures] and words or both. You can use these ideas in your story or can just use your own ideas. The choice is yours and you should decide this reasonably quickly so you can begin to write. You won't lose marks for using your own ideas.

Pay attention to all the instructions and use your planning time well. The instructions on the test may tell you to think about the characters you will use, the complication or problem and the end. It will also tell you to write in sentences, pay attention to vocabulary, spelling and punctuation. An instruction may also be that your work may be published so that you need to edit carefully.

Remember in the test you will have five (5) minutes of planning time. Then you will have thirty (30) minutes to write the narrative. Finally you will have five (5) minutes to edit your work. The editing process is important and you should use this time to check your work including spelling and punctuation. One easy structural thing to check is paragraphs. Look at your work to see if you have forgotten to use them in your rush to write your piece.

What Markers Look For When Examining Your Work

Of course your test will be marked and so it is good to know what the examiner or marker is looking for. Currently there are ten (10) criteria that are used for marking the writing task. These are shown below with the mark or score range shown for each one listed below.

☑	Audience	0-6
☑	Text structure	0-4
☑	Ideas	0-5
☑	Character and setting	0-4
☑	Vocabulary	0-5
☑	Cohesion	0-4
☑	Paragraphing	0-2
☑	Sentence structure	0-6
☑	Punctuation	0-5
☑	Spelling	0-6

Most of these terms are self explanatory but the term cohesion just means that your story holds together with one idea or line of thought. As you get older you will see the term 'sustained writing' which means much the same thing.

By understanding clearly the information you have just read you will have taken the first major step on your path to success in these tests. By knowing what you have to do you will be prepared for it and confident in what you need to do to succeed. Re-read these introductory notes several times. Then you know what to expect in the exam and won't be surprised by the words in the exam or the format. The next section gives you some writing tips to help improve your writing.

IMPROVING YOUR WRITING

Writing improvement is a matter of practice and developing your skills and vocabulary so you can express yourself clearly.

Writing the Correct Text Type

When you are asked to write in a particular text type make sure that you follow the correct structure or format for that type of writing. For example in a narrative you would use the structure: orientation, complication and resolution. Try to know all the different types and what is required. This book will help you to do that.

Ensuring Cohesion

To ensure that your story sticks together it is best to have one idea that holds the story together. If you have too many ideas your story will become confused and so will your readers or audience. Remember to stick to the topic or idea you are given in the stimulus material for the exam. Make sure the tense of the story is consistent and you have sustained the main idea.

Write in Paragraphs

One of the marking criteria for the exam is paragraphing and you should begin a new paragraph for a new thought or concept in your story. Shorter paragraphs are usually clearer and audiences like to be clear on what they are reading. If you get to the end of your story and begin to edit and notice you don't have paragraphs you can still put them in. to do this you can just put a [symbol before the word where a new paragraph starts. The marker will understand what you mean.

Engaging the Audience

To engage and entertain an audience a good introduction is necessary. It needs to be interesting and make the audience want to read on. You can practice this by writing different introductions to the same story and seeing which one your family and friends like best. The same idea is also relevant to the resolution. Audiences don't like stories which don't have an ending that solves the puzzle or complication in the story. Use the planning time to work out your ending.

Vocabulary

Vocabulary is a powerful tool for the writer to have. Word choices help expression and make your idea(s) easy for the audience to understand. To improve your vocabulary you can use a dictionary and a thesaurus to find new words. Make sure you understand what a word means before you use it and also how to use it correctly. Don't just use 'big' words to impress.

Sentence Structure

When you write your work make sure you write in sentences. As you learn to write you will use longer or compound sentences. Sentences should begin with a capital letter and end with a piece of punctuation such as a full stop or question mark. This will help the marker know you can use a sentence.

Spelling

Spelling is something that can be practiced if you are not as strong in this area as you might be. Word lists can be useful and there are many good spelling books that can assist you in developing your skills. Don't be afraid to use new words as you can correct spelling in the editing process.

Characters

Characters are usually the people in your story. For a short story such as the one in the test you should not have too many characters. This is because you need to make sure your audience can follow a few characters without becoming lost. You can then also develop them better by using description and dialogue.

Setting

Setting is the place where your story happens. A story may have more than one setting. For example you could be out on a bushwalk in a forest and then travel home in a car. You should describe your setting so the audience know where they are and can imagine it more clearly. The markers will be looking that you have a setting so ensure your story has a place.

Editing

The editing process is an important one and you have five (5) minutes at the end of the test to edit. In your mind you should have a mental list of the areas the examiners are looking for and work on those. Think of things like tense and ask the question does my story have the correct structure. Re-read your work and fix little errors in the spelling, punctuation and grammar that may occur under exam conditions.

WRITING A NARRATIVE

The basic structure of a narrative is shown below:orientation [introduction]
complication [problem]
resolution [conclusion]

Each of these MUST be included in your narrative or story. It is particularly important to have a strong introduction and resolution to

leave your audience satisfied at the end of their reading. Remember that the purpose of a narrative is firstly to entertain but it can also inform, persuade and emotionally touch the audience.

In clarifying your thoughts on the structure an orientation tells the audience the WHO, WHERE and WHEN of the story while the complication is the problem that arises in the narrative. An orientation sentence might be: Sybil was walking along a winding, dirt track in the National Park west of Sydney.

The resolution or conclusion to your story needs to have a solution to the complication you have created. A complication to our story might be an unexpected storm that traps Sybil and the resolution might be her rescue by helicopter. The complication usually leads to the climax or most exciting part of the story.

The audience need to be engaged with the story and one way to do this is to have characters that the audience like. If they like your characters they will read on to find out what happens to them. To ensure your characters are engaging or interesting they need to share with the reader some feelings and thoughts. As a writer you can do this by using description and/ or dialogue (conversation). If you can't think of a good description just use someone you know who might be like that character. With dialogue or conversation ensure that they speak correctly for their age.

It is important to focus on one main idea or theme in the story so as to remain consistent throughout the narrative. This will stop you and the audience becoming confused about a number of ideas. The planning time before you begin writing will help you decide on your idea and plan how you will maintain it. You only have thirty minutes to write so don't plan for too many characters and think about your resolution so you don't have to rush the ending and spoil the story.

The writing hints in the previous section apply here as well so you should check all those items in your editing. These include: spelling, punctuation. grammar, sentence structure, paragraphing, setting, character and cohesion.

LOST

You are about to write a story or narrative. The idea for your work is 'LOST'.

Many things can be lost including people, objects and memories. Some lost things are found and some are lost forever. Lost items can be searched for or we may never know they are lost. Some words to help you with your story are: **misinformed**, **treacherous** and **deception**.

Think About
- Your characters and setting
- The complication or conflict in your story
- Your resolution or end
- Who will read your story

Remember to:
- Plan your story before writing
- Use sentences
- Use well chosen words
- Watch spelling and punctuation
- Check your work carefully
- Edit carefully

GET LOST

1. Lost

Introduction
The orientation or introduction has the who, when and where of the story and a hint at the complication. Here it is the background which sets the scene

"I've never lost anything," said Grandpa as he was sitting in the old garden shed where we were doing some winter chores, "but I have misplaced a few things for a long time".

It was a happy day for us as it was the last hours we had together before he went into hospital for the final time. I always remembered the times we had in that shed and the things that he taught me both about gardening and life. Many of my holidays had been spent on the old farm because my parents had divorced and often they had to work through the school holidays. I was shipped off, not unwillingly, to the grandparents. The farm had plenty to occupy a teenage boy and despite the age difference I had a great many grand holidays there.

Here the plot begins to unfold.

Sets scene for the complication

Now I was back as an adult as I had been on and off for years but this was a sadder time. I was helping Gran go through all the old things now the farmhouse and property was being sold off. After Grandpa's death it was too hard for her to manage it all and it was time to move on. We had covered most of the house and all the rooms had been cleared. We had certainly found some of the things that had been misplaced as Grandpa would say over years but nothing spectacular.

As I rolled the carpet mat up in the old study I found an old trap door. Intrigued I called to Gran and told her my discovery.

"No mystery there" she told me. "The old cellar hasn't been used since my mother's younger days. We didn't need it anymore because of the electricity and such. I'm not even sure that the ladder is still attached to get down. It's only tiny anyway – dug out of the earth."

"May I have a look?"

"Of course," she replied smiling ay my naïve curiosity. "I don't think there's any danger there."

Complication.
Here it is finding of the old cellar and the possibility of finding something secret.Note how the tension builds to the resolution. The suspense keeps the reader interested

I opened up the door by turning the simple ringlock and pulled up the hinged flooring. Their was a musty smell but it wasn't that unpleasant. It was very dark and I went to the ute for a torch. Gran waited patiently for my return and warned me to be careful as I shone the torch into the darkness. The cellar was very tiny and lined with simple wooden shelving most of which was empty. A few old Vacola preserving jars lay around but they too were empty.

Shining the strong beam around I looked for something special without any success. I looked at the ladder and decided to go in and have a closer look. I heeded Gran's advice and was careful but the steps were still strong. Looking

Note how the tension builds to the resolution. The suspense keeps the reader interested

Resolution
Here the story ends with an ambivalent ending. A resolution can be negative or positive

around I went two or three steps to the end of the cramped cellar. I turned around and under the end shelf on the back wall was a small brown suitcase. It was one of those old school bags that were no longer used by anyone. I grabbed it and called out to Gran about my find.

She waited for me and I emerged from the cellar clutching my find. I imagined all sorts of riches and secrets in the bag. Even Gran said she had never seen it and had no idea of what might be in it. I shut off the torch and put the bag on the floor.

"Would you like to open it?" I asked her. "It may contain treasures or secrets."

"No, you do it. I have no ambition in that direction," she said cryptically.

I leant forward in anticipation and clicked the two old locks. The lid can away freely in my hand. I could only feel disappointment. It was empty.

"Lost time is never found again" she said. "Let's get back to it."

She sounded just like Grandpa I thought fleetingly and warmly as I turned to finish the job.

VOYAGE

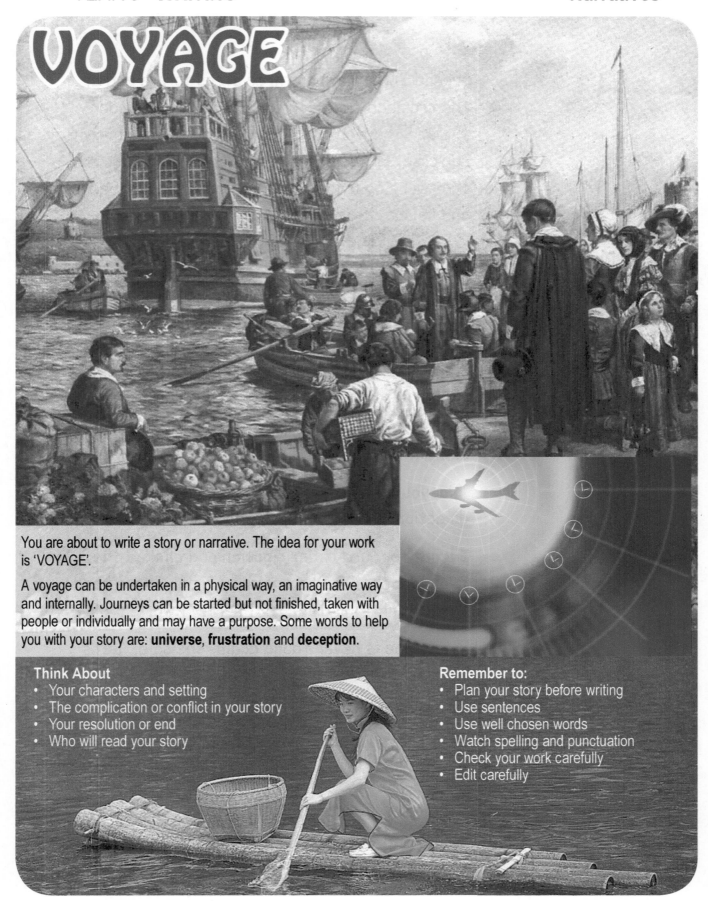

You are about to write a story or narrative. The idea for your work is 'VOYAGE'.

A voyage can be undertaken in a physical way, an imaginative way and internally. Journeys can be started but not finished, taken with people or individually and may have a purpose. Some words to help you with your story are: **universe**, **frustration** and **deception**.

Think About
- Your characters and setting
- The complication or conflict in your story
- Your resolution or end
- Who will read your story

Remember to:
- Plan your story before writing
- Use sentences
- Use well chosen words
- Watch spelling and punctuation
- Check your work carefully
- Edit carefully

2. Voyage

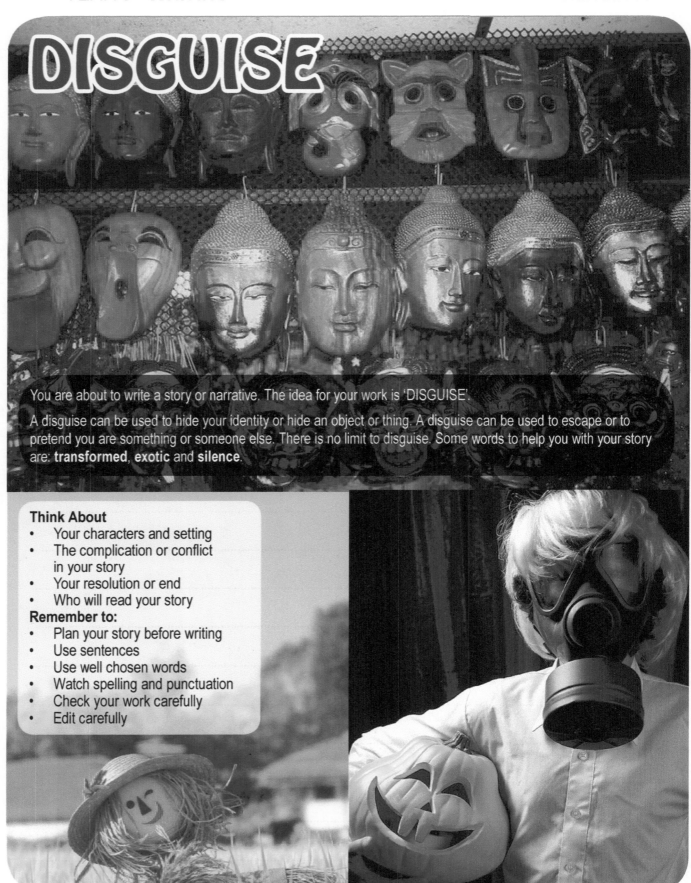

DISGUISE

You are about to write a story or narrative. The idea for your work is 'DISGUISE'.

A disguise can be used to hide your identity or hide an object or thing. A disguise can be used to escape or to pretend you are something or someone else. There is no limit to disguise. Some words to help you with your story are: **transformed**, **exotic** and **silence**.

Think About
*   Your characters and setting
*   The complication or conflict in your story
*   Your resolution or end
*   Who will read your story

Remember to:
*   Plan your story before writing
*   Use sentences
*   Use well chosen words
*   Watch spelling and punctuation
*   Check your work carefully
*   Edit carefully

4 Disguise

....

....

....

....

....

....

....

....

....

....

....

....

....

....

....

....

....

You are about to write a story or narrative. The idea for your work is 'MESSAGE'.

Messages can be between people, races, animals or machines. They can be used to solve or cause problems. Messages can go astray or be misinterpreted. They can be in any language, shape and form. Some words to help you with your story are: **confused**, **unexpected** and **castle**.

Just be yourself: you are wonderful

 No Trespassing

Think About
- Your characters and setting
- The complication or conflict in your story
- Your resolution or end
- Who will read your story

Remember to:
- Plan your story before writing
- Use sentences
- Use well chosen words
- Watch spelling and punctuation
- Check your work carefully
- Edit carefully

MESSAGE

5. Message

....

....

....

....

....

....

....

....

....

....

....

....

....

....

....

....

© Alfred Fletcher
Coroneos Publications

You are about to write a story or narrative. The idea for your work is 'EXERCISE'.

Exercise has become part of many people's lives and you can exercise in many ways. We are often told that exercise is good for people but also other living things like our pets. Exercise can cause injuries. Some words to help you with your story are: **achievement**, **false** and **mountain**.

Think About
- Your characters and setting
- The complication or conflict in your story
- Your resolution or end
- Who will read your story

Remember to:
- Plan your story before writing
- Use sentences
- Use well chosen words
- Watch spelling and punctuation
- Check your work carefully
- Edit carefully

5 Exercise

OCEAN

You are about to write a story or narrative. The idea for your work is 'OCEAN'.

Oceans cover much of the Earth's surface and contain many different life forms. Many parts of the ocean are unexplored and extremely deep. The ocean can be a place to enjoy but it also holds many dangers. Some words to help you with your story are: **illegal**, **fathom** and **squall**.

Think About
- Your characters and setting
- The complication or conflict in your story
- Your resolution or end
- Who will read your story

Remember to:
- Plan your story before writing
- Use sentences
- Use well chosen words
- Watch spelling and punctuation
- Check your work carefully
- Edit carefully

6. Ocean

HYSTERIA

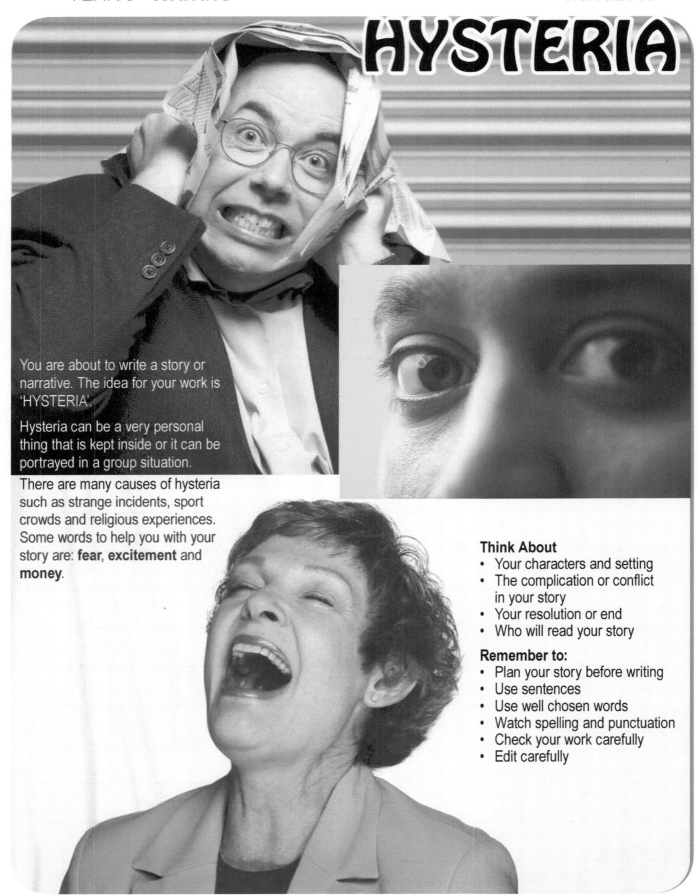

You are about to write a story or narrative. The idea for your work is 'HYSTERIA'.

Hysteria can be a very personal thing that is kept inside or it can be portrayed in a group situation.

There are many causes of hysteria such as strange incidents, sport crowds and religious experiences. Some words to help you with your story are: **fear**, **excitement** and **money**.

Think About
- Your characters and setting
- The complication or conflict in your story
- Your resolution or end
- Who will read your story

Remember to:
- Plan your story before writing
- Use sentences
- Use well chosen words
- Watch spelling and punctuation
- Check your work carefully
- Edit carefully

7. Hysteria

SUCCESS

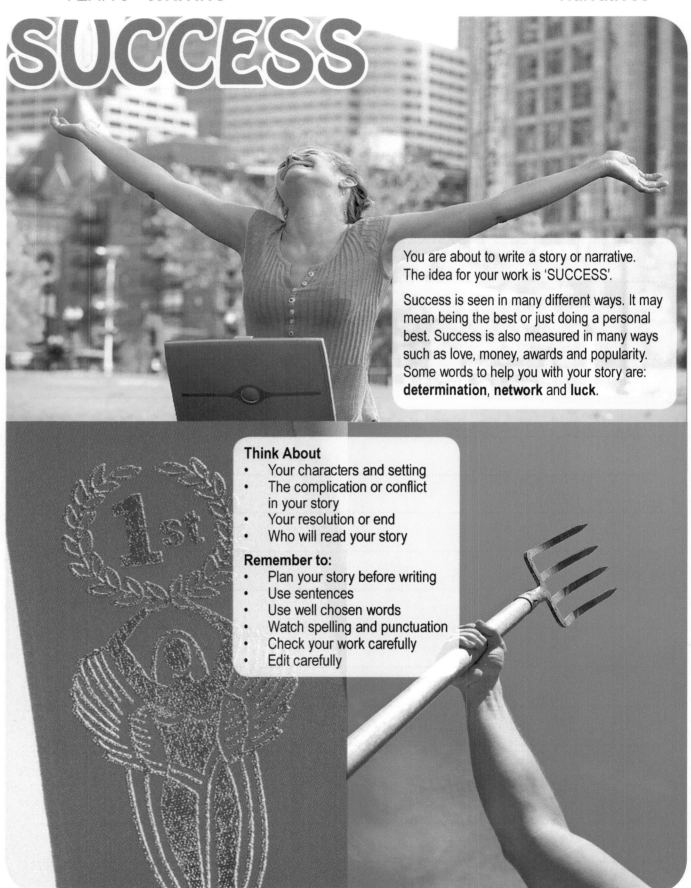

You are about to write a story or narrative. The idea for your work is 'SUCCESS'.

Success is seen in many different ways. It may mean being the best or just doing a personal best. Success is also measured in many ways such as love, money, awards and popularity. Some words to help you with your story are: **determination**, **network** and **luck**.

Think About
- Your characters and setting
- The complication or conflict in your story
- Your resolution or end
- Who will read your story

Remember to:
- Plan your story before writing
- Use sentences
- Use well chosen words
- Watch spelling and punctuation
- Check your work carefully
- Edit carefully

8. Success

....

....

....

....

....

....

....

....

....

....

....

....

....

....

....

....

RESTAURANT

You are about to write a story or narrative. The idea for your work is 'RESTAURANT'.

Restaurant's serve all kinds of food, have different interiors and levels of service. The customers are varied and anyone can go into a restaurant. The staff service can be great or terrible but chefs can be dramatic. Some words to help you with your story are: **wholesome**, **pungent** and **criminal**.

Think About
- Your characters and setting
- The complication or conflict in your story
- Your resolution or end
- Who will read your story

Remember to:
- Plan your story before writing
- Use sentences
- Use well chosen words
- Watch spelling and punctuation
- Check your work carefully
- Edit carefully

9. Restaurant

MATURITY

You are about to write a story or narrative. The idea for your work is 'MATURITY'.

Maturity is about growing up and getting wiser at the the same time. Young people are always told to be mature but it is not just people that mature. Wine, cheese and other foods do as well. Some words to help you with your story are: **fountain**, **righteousness** and **conflict**.

Think About
- Your characters and setting
- The complication or conflict in your story
- Your resolution or end
- Who will read your story

Remember to:
- Plan your story before writing
- Use sentences
- Use well chosen words
- Watch spelling and punctuation
- Check your work carefully
- Edit carefully

10. Maturity

....

....

....

....

....

....

....

....

....

....

....

....

....

....

....

....

....

CHALLENGE

You are about to write a story or narrative. The idea for your work is 'CHALLENGE'.

Challenges can be many things and come in many ways. Challenges can be overcome or they can overcome individuals or groups of people. Many people enjoy challenges while they destroy others. Some words to help you with your story are: **confront**, **devious** and **pinnacle**.

Think About
- Your characters and setting
- The complication or conflict in your story
- Your resolution or end
- Who will read your story

Remember to:
- Plan your story before writing
- Use sentences
- Use well chosen words
- Watch spelling and punctuation
- Check your work carefully
- Edit carefully

11. Growth

....

....

....

....

....

....

....

....

....

....

....

....

....

....

....

....

DEVELOPMENT

You are about to write a story or narrative. The idea for your work is 'DEVELOPMENT;.

A development can be many things such as a construction site or a personal development. The word is about change and developments can be threatening to some and welcome to others. Some words to help you with your story are: **uncertainty**, **constrain** and **valley**.

Think About
- Your characters and setting
- The complication or conflict in your story
- Your resolution or end
- Who will read your story

Remember to:
- Plan your story before writing
- Use sentences
- Use well chosen words
- Watch spelling and punctuation
- Check your work carefully
- Edit carefully

12: Development

....

....

....

....

....

....

....

....

....

....

....

....

....

....

....

L'ARTILLERIE CONTRE LA GRÊLE

EXPERIMENT

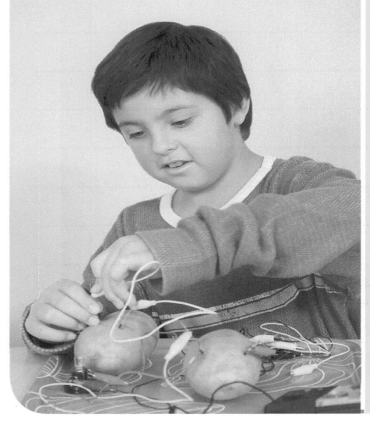

You are about to write a story or narrative. The idea for your work is 'EXPERIMENT'.

Scientists are not the only people who experiment. People experiment every day when they try something new to see if it works. Some experiments fail and others change the world both for better and worse. Some words to help you with your story are: **time**, **defender** and **salt**.

Think About
- Your characters and setting
- The complication or conflict in your story
- Your resolution or end
- Who will read your story

Remember to:
- Plan your story before writing
- Use sentences
- Use well chosen words
- Watch spelling and punctuation
- Check your work carefully
- Edit carefully

13. Experiment

© Alfred Fletcher
Coroneos Publications

You are about to write a story or narrative. The idea for your work is 'ROAD'.

Roads can be found anywhere and can be small tracks to huge superhighways. They may not even be on Earth. Roads can be made from many substances and built for different purposes. Some words to help you with your story are: **rugged**, **water** and **satisfaction**.

Think About
- Your characters and setting
- The complication or conflict in your story
- Your resolution or end
- Who will read your story

Remember to:
- Plan your story before writing
- Use Sentences
- Use well chosen words
- Watch spelling and Punctuation
- Check your work carefully
- Edit carefully

14. Road

....

....

....

....

....

....

....

....

....

....

....

....

....

....

....

....

© Alfred Fletcher
Coroneos Publications

ADVENTURE

You are about to write a story or narrative. The idea for your work is 'ADVENTURE'.

An adventure can take you many places but can also be close to home. Adventures can create heroes and save worlds but also lead to failure and misery. Adventures can be fun and exciting but also dangerous. Some words to help you with your story are: **excavation**, **insurance** and **expedient**.

Think About
* Your characters and setting
* The complication or conflict in your story
* Your resolution or end
* Who will read your story

Remember to:
* Plan your story before writing
* Use sentences
* Use well chosen words
* Watch spelling and punctuation
* Check your work carefully
* Edit carefully

15 Adventure

....

....

....

....

....

....

....

....

....

....

....

....

....

....

....

....

1. Lost

"I've never lost anything," said Grandpa as he was sitting in the old garden shed where we were doing some winter chores, "but I have misplaced a few things for a long time".

It was a happy day for us as it was the last hours we had together before he went into hospital for the final time. I always remembered the times we had in that shed and the things that he taught me both about gardening and life. Many of my holidays had been spent on the old farm because my parents had divorced and often they had to work through the school holidays. I was shipped off, not unwillingly, to the grandparents. The farm had plenty to occupy a teenage boy and despite the age difference I had a great many grand holidays there.

Now I was back as an adult as I had been on and off for years but this was a sadder time. I was helping Gran go through all the old things now the farmhouse and property was being sold off. After Grandpa's death it was too hard for her to manage it all and it was time to move on. We had covered most of the house and all the rooms had been cleared. We had certainly found some of the things that had been misplaced as Grandpa would say over years but nothing spectacular.

As I rolled the carpet mat up in the old study I found an old trap door. Intrigued I called to Gran and told her my discovery.

"No mystery there" she told me. "The old cellar hasn't been used since my mother's younger days. We didn't need it anymore because of the electricity and such. I'm not even sure that the ladder is still attached to get down. It's only tiny anyway – dug out of the earth."

"May I have a look?"

"Of course," she replied smiling ay my naïve curiosity. "I don't think there's any danger there."

I opened up the door by turning the simple ringlock and pulled up the hinged flooring. Their was a musty smell but it wasn't that unpleasant. It was very dark and I went to the ute for a torch. Gran waited patiently for my return and warned me to be careful as I shone the torch into the darkness. The cellar was very tiny and lined with simple wooden shelving most of which was empty. A few old Vacola preserving jars lay around but they too were empty.

Shining the strong beam around I looked for something special without any success. I looked at the ladder and decided to go in and have a closer look. I heeded Gran's advice and was careful but the steps were still strong. Looking around I went two or three steps to the end of the cramped cellar. I turned around and under the end shelf on the back wall was a small brown suitcase. It was one of those old school bags that were no longer used by anyone. I grabbed it and called out to Gran about my find.

She waited for me and I emerged from the cellar clutching my find. I imagined all sorts of riches and secrets in the bag. Even Gran said she had never seen it and had no idea of what might be in it. I shut off the torch and put the bag on the floor.

"Would you like yo open it?" I asked her. "It may contain treasures or secrets."

"No, you do it. I have no ambition in that direction," she said cryptically.

I leant forward in anticipation and clicked the two old locks. The lid can away freely in my hand. I could only feel disappointment. It was empty.

"Lost time is never found again" she said. "Let's get back to it."

She sounded just like Grandpa I thought fleetingly and warmly as I turned to finish the job.

2. Voyage

Captain Ahab Jones was a man not used to frustration. Would the tide never turn he thought as his ship, The Unicorn, wallowed in the harbour waiting to sail. His cargo was bound for the Javanese coast where he would return to England with spices that would make him even wealthier than he was now. He didn't have to go but he loved the long voyages across oceans and thrived on the all male atmosphere of the ship. The ship was his universe he was sole master and commander.

Hours later the tide turned and the current began to rush through the channel to the ocean beyond. The Unicorn was sluggish with her heavy load of garments from the mills and the men worked hard to get the ship around and under sail. Jones watched with pleasure as his men worked smoothly and competently without much instruction. He knew he had a good crew and paid them well. Many had been with him for years and it was a situation of mutual trust. While some sailors still worried they could sail off the edge of the world he had no such illusions.

The motion of the ship soon reassured him and he went below decks to chart a course. The journey was uneventful with the trade route a well known path across the seas. The Javanese coast was a different story with Dutch traders trying to sink British ships and only a few British trading posts supported by soldiers amidst a hostile native population and jungle. This was his busiest time and where he earned his money. As the clung to the coast line and rounded the point he soon saw a problem. The trading post was a smoking wreck and it seemed freshly destroyed although abandoned by people.

He put in a long boat and went ashore himself to investigate. The place was destroyed and many bodies lay where they had fallen. He was just about to make a move back to The Unicorn when four bedraggled men came out of the jungle. These four were the only survivors of the Dutch attack and had escaped into the jungle and hidden. Jones was told that three ships had come and bombarded before a landing party had finished them off. Unworried he took them all back to the ship and headed off to the main British settlement.

Three leagues on he rounded Cape George and saw three Dutch frigates moving leeward to begin attack. The Unicorn had few guns but Jones had the element of surprise. He rounded the boat to starboard and headed in. The men were primed and began firing canons at the Dutch as soon as they were in range. The battle was short with two Dutch ships floundered and the other running for deep water. The men cheered but Jones was focused on his cargo which was still intact. He moved toward his anchor point and began to plan the cargo exchange. His journey would be profitable despite these problems and that is what mattered to him.

3. Disguise

The dark laneway helped the perfect disguise of Alan Free as he moved slowly toward the darkened doorway of the underground café. It was an exotic meeting place for the bohemian crowd that was left under the strict communist regime in East Germany. Here meeting his contact was a risk because the secret police probably monitored the café but he needed the information quickly and badly. He needed to know if his team of informants had been compromised.

His disguise was as a cabaret performer and he hoped that the drag outfit underneath his bulky overcoat would be enough to ensure his quick exit should trouble arise. His face was known to the communist authorities but not with all this make-up on. He smiled at the doorman who grunted at him but did allow entry. Inside the lighting was dull but the noise was intense as the performers on the small stage competed with the sounds of conversation and food being eaten. Alan took off his overcoat and was glad he was in drag as he looked just like most of the crowd.

Grabbing a table in the corner he sat, ordered a drink and waited for his contact. A youngish girl soon sat opposite him dressed in a man's dinner suit. Tina still looked great he thought to himself but instantly corrected himself and got back to business. She leaned across to him and whispered in her ear like they were lovers but she just had one word, 'compromised'. His heart sank and he knew that his time under cover was over and began mentally to plan his escape and how he would help his people if they hadn't been taken already. The East Germans weren't known for their fair treatment of prisoners and murdered as freely as they drank schnapps.

Tina squeezed his hand as she got up to leave and he wished he could do more for her. To leave her would mean her death eventually. Just then he heard sirens and the sound of scuffling at the front of the room. It was a police raid on the club he hoped as he headed for the side door. He saw Tina shoved over a table by others rushing to escape and went back to get her. Hauling her to her feet he grabbed her hand and jumped on the stage as the police came rushing in. He followed the crowd who were heading for the back stage area door. Here they were grabbed by the police and roughed up. Held by a cordon of police he knew he was trapped and wished he was armed.

The sergeant came over and began to hit people with a truncheon for fun. As he worked his way along the line Alan had to restrain himself as the man hit Tina and himself several times. The sergeant even spat on him as said, 'Degenerate'. At least my disguise works Alan thought as he bled slowly from a head wound. The sergeant told his men to let them all go as their were no infiltrators in this crowd of scum.

Now all Alan had to do was get Tina and himself across the border to the West. There was always another problem when you were a spy.

4. Message

The siege seemed to have lasted an eternity and had been so unexpected the people in the castle had been confused and unprepared. After years of peaceful co-existence the Morth had decide to attack and lay siege to the Quillian castle. This castle was the seat of power for the Quillian kingdom and for it to fall was unthinkable but that was what was happening. With all the troops trapped inside and being whittled away by the constant bombardment from the catapults camped around the castle.

Inside things were becoming dire. The water was fine as the wells had a never-ending supply but food was an issue for the large population that had flooded in just before the gates were shut to reject the on-coming forces. Most of the grain was gone and their were no animals left except for the horses which would be needed for battle. The peasants were even eating rat when they could get it. King Jonah was more than concerned and wondered where his son was. Prince Esau had been trapped outside by the sudden onslaught as he was visiting some outlying villages. Nothing had been heard from him for three months and it was assumed he had been murdered by the Morth.

It seemed the castle could only last another week or two before they would have to open the gates and attack in a final effort to be free. They had little hope but it was a chance. Preparations began and swords and arrows sharpened. King Jonah moved around the castle talking to his people and encouraging them. He was a man of the people despite his title and they loved and respected him. Many expressed sorrow for the loss of his son but he told them to look to the future. Plans were laid for an attack on the morrow but when dawn came the command was for the remaining troops and armed civilians to stand down.

Confusion reigned and many were alarmed by the change in tactics. Some were relieved that they had escaped death but felt the order had only delayed the inevitable. New orders were issued and the attack was reset for two days hence. Preparations began again and as the nights passed a general feeling of apprehension could be felt amongst the people. Around four just before the dawn the signal was given to move to the keep area for the opening of the gates and drawbridge. Horses snorted as the picked up on the fear of the men. The King moved to the front of the lines and they all gained reassurance from this confident move.

The men could see smoke from the enemy camp looming over the castle wall and they knew the Morth were prepared for them. As the gates opened they were stilled by the sight before them. The enemy camp was on fire and the catapults torched. Chaos was the catchword in the Morth camp and the King cried to his men to attack. As they stormed mercilessly into the Morth camp the men raised a cheer as Prince Esau appeared with a small band of men. The King thanked Esau for the pigeon message that held the attack until his saboteurs could wreck havoc. Victory was assured and swift. Quillian was safe again.

5. Exercise

Jennifer had been a physiotherapist for about ten years and was getting tired of fixing people who could have prevented their injuries with some thought and preparation. All that yelling and push, push, push at the gym was doing more damage than good as unfit and overweight people tried to get the perfect body in a week. While she was well paid for her work Jennifer felt she had achieved all she could in her current job and was looking for a new challenge. Deciding to break free from her daily grind she thought about a challenge that would change her life.

Jennifer began to read and investigate some of the great adventures and challenges left in the world. She explored avenues by researching what others had tried to achieve and eventually decided upon an assault on the Big Seven. This was an ambitious project for someone who had never climbed before but it was a challenge that would consume the next decade. The Big Seven Mountains were a challenge that would take her to every continent. Jennifer planned to climb Aconcagua (South America), Carstensz Pyramid (Oceania), Denali (North America), Elbrus (Europe), Everest (Asia), Kilimanjaro (Africa) and Vinson (Antarctica).

She immediately began to plan and started a rigorous plan of training and exercise. She started to attend rock climbing schools and do Pilates to develop her core strength. After about six months she went o her first real climb just a simple summer walk up Mount Kosciusko in the Snowy Mountains of New South Wales. It went well and she was thrilled. Jennifer continued to train and she was focused on her goal. She knew only one hundred people had ever achieved this goal and many had died in the attempt. She was making no false claims, it was dangerous, but it was something she had to do.

Her first target would be Mount Kilimanjaro which was the simplest climb technically. Her trip was planned to the last detail and when she took of from Adelaide Airport she knew her dream was in full motion. Africa was strange to her but with her focus on one thing it all became a blur.

The climbing companions were all enjoying themselves but she was very focused and uptight all the way to the summit. Once Jennifer was on the summit alone she was exhilarated and felt that all her hard work had been worthwhile.

Back home in Torrens she began to plan her next summit which was Mount Elbrus in Russia and seventeen thousand foot climb. This was not a difficult climb either and one she felt was attainable. Jennifer's main goal was the ultimate climb on the ultimate mountain, Everest. This would be the make or break climb and she would be prepared. Jennifer planned to write about her experiences and teach people how to exercise properly so they wouldn't injure themselves. All her dreams seemed so close now. Jennifer thought how pleased she was that she had decided to follow her dream.

6. Ocean

The idea of doing anything illegal appealed to Captain Cowes who had turned from trader to the more profitable and dangerous career of pirate. He loved the thrill of the chase, the battle and the booty. Not for him the hidden treasure, he stole it and spent it at one of the less populated ports along the African coast. Many of his crew were African slaves freed because he had sunk the ships taking them from their land and they loved him for it. These were men he could trust and trust was unusual in the pirate business. The last of the crew had returned to the Cutty Shark from time onshore and they had returned penniless. It was now time to move on and get some more booty.

Sailing west Cowes told the crew that they would now target some of the merchant ships heading back to Europe from Durban which would be loaded with goods and perhaps even some fine food and liquor. The ship sailed along the coast, just out of sight of the shoreline. Many eyes watched for boats like the Cutty Shark for the Navy ships who would give anything to trap a pirate ship that caused them so much grief. Cowes turned into Rhodesia Bay and which gave him good seaward vision and waited to spot a ship sailing for Europe. He thought their was no point in wandering the ocean for nothing. He even sent men ashore to refill their water supplies.

About a week later just when the men were getting restless Cowes spotted a large schooner sitting low in the water and heading north. He gave them some space and then hauled anchor fast. He wanted to catch them in the dark of night and attack early in the morning. This had always worked before and saw no reason to change. The men worked ceaselessly to keep the Cutty Shark trim into the wind and they made good pace. They knew their would be no rest for the next twenty-four hours. It would be even longer for late in the night they were hit by a squall form the south and the boat was driven hard in the churning seas.

Coming out of this into the dawn they saw their prey wallowing with a broken mast in the ocean. Drawing close the other boat could do nothing as the pirates boarded and began to steal everything they could. Not a shot was fired as they stripped the other ship clean and left the crew and astounded passengers standing on the deck. Cowes looked at the flabbergasted group and laughing told them he was a gentleman and no harm would come to them despite his reputation. He knew he was no gentleman but this was so easy he could afford to be. He thought they would all be dead now if it wasn't for the mast broken in that squall.

His crew untied the ships and Cowes waved goodbye to the stranded ship. Some of the amazed passengers even waved back as if they were friends but the other crew didn't look so impressed by his gesture. His crew was in a good mood and looked forward to spending their ill gotten gains at the next port. Settling back into his captain's chair Cowes thought what a good life was had by being a pirate.

7. Hysteria

The Global Financial Crisis had created a real hysteria in the money men of Wall Street. Kenwin Franklin had never felt so much fear and exhilaration in the space of so short a time. He was amazed at the amount of trading that had gone on in the stock market for the last week and glad he had been smart enough to cash in a month before. He had seen the signs as he had sold many of the toxic mortgages that had destroyed the markets. He loved he had won and was prepared to now sit out the pain while those around him fell. His company had always steered clear of reinsuring and was well cashed up. No hysteria here just a gloating calm.

Kenwin wondered what he would do next as he needed the thrill of the deal to make him feel alive. Only he and one other man, Warren 'Rabbits' Feast III, had the resources to capitalise on the misery out there. Kenwin hated 'Rabbits' more than anything because the people loved his common touch and hated Kenwin because he lived a rich and extravagant lifestyle everyone could be envious of. Heading home in the limo Kenwin wondered if he began a Vulture Fund in the morning he could start buying up distressed companies and resell them at a profit when things turned around. This comforting thought occupied his night hours.

The next morning in his palatial penthouse office their was some bad news awaiting him. Some investors had been cashing in their company bonds and others been wanting to withdraw their investments. He thought an announcement would calm the markets and it did for a short time but he became aware that rumours were going around the city business district that his Fund was in trouble. He was furious and went on a media blitz to reassure investors but the selling continued. Kenwin was concerned now and angry when he discovered that one of his subsidiaries had been balancing the books by selling reinsurance for C class mortgages. He'd missed this and was more angry at himself than the acolyte who thought he was doing him a favour. Kenwin would let him go in a week or two.

More and more bad news kept piling in and the Fund began to feel the pressure on its cash flow. Never borrow long term with short term money his first boss had told him and it turned out to be true. He felt their was no way out except Government bail-out and that was unlikely for a man of his reputation. The Franklin Fund was near insolvent when Kenwin received a call. He was shocked to learn from his secretary that it was 'Rabbits' Feast III on the line.

'Rabbits' was quick to say that he was offering to buy Franklin out for ten cents in the dollar. Kenwin went hysterical at this and screamed down the phone. 'Rabbits' then told him that he was the architect of his demise and had bought all the reinsurance paper and wanted what was his. Kenwin's hysteria amplified and he saw no way out. His greed had made him what he was and then destroyed him. He felt real fear for the first time before gathering himself and swearing vengeance on the man who had caused his fall.

8. Success

My father always told me that the only place success came before work was in the dictionary and it seemed that his advice was completely wrong despite his good education and work ethic. I had made my own way in the world through luck and the ability to network with the right people. The person who helped me most was the Devil. Yes, I had sold my soul but it was certainly worth it.

I had everything I could want and more. For one simple deal I had become the richest man in the world with all I could desire. Through my vast wealth I had made connections which made me even more money. My father also said money didn't make you happy but I had also proven that old cliché incorrect. My life was a fantasy, my every whim catered for and I didn't have to pay the piper until I passed away. Well, who cares when you're dead?

My life went on like this for years and I never saw or heard from the Devil during this time. At times I even forgot about him and the deal I had made. As I grew older I became a little more responsible and even married, actually I married a few times and had several children all of whom loved my money and the things that it bought. I wondered if I should have gone for the eternal life option but it was never offered and I wondered what eternal damnation might belike or if it existed at all.

My plan from that point became clear, how could I cheat the Devil and make it the deal of a lifetime? I began to consider options and set many of my underlings to investigate any and every possibility. I loved my wealth too much to repent and who knew when your deathbed was likely to occur so that option was out. If I didn't die he couldn't get my soul. Their was no statute of limitations on the deal so I had to cheat death somehow. For years nothing positive seemed to offer itself but I kept pouring resources into it. The more I researched the more I began to regret the deal. Eternity seemed a long time when you are getting older.

Everything seemed impossible as the years went on and I even financed an expedition to search for the Holy Grail without success.

I definitely needed luck and technology came to the rescue. The developing science of cryogenics seemed to offer some respite if not total success. I helped develop new techniques and created a system where a human body could be frozen and life maintained while the brain remained active. I would be frozen alive but would have to stay that way until something else turned up.

It was all planned for my hundredth birthday and the deal was done. I went into the chamber and was frozen by the computer controlled systems that had back-up and failsafe. My mind was still alert and after an hour or so I began to get bored. After two hours I was very bored. After three hours I was getting restless and wanted out but was stuck. A week later I was near insanity and all I could hear was laughter and a voice saying welcome to eternal damnation!

9. Restaurant

Tony 'Big Boss' Giglioni had always loved Sonny's Italian Restaurant and ate spaghetti and meatballs there every Friday night with his entourage. Sonny initially welcomed his patronage as it was a new business but as time moved on the reputation Tony had was putting customers off. This was especially so recently the new gang wars had broken out amongst the families and Tony's entourage had grown into twenty or so heavily armed goons that came with the three or four Capo's who came to eat.

Sonny knew he couldn't do anything and didn't even think about it. Friday nights became a closed restaurant night and everyone had the meatballs. Sonny always cooked the meal himself and employed no staff except his wife to wait on them. Tony payed well and this was some compensation for his effort. To his discomfort Sonny became known as 'The Chef to the Mafia'.

One Friday Tony arrived with the usual fanfare and things were in full swing when the sound of sirens could be heard drawing closer. Tony sighed and assumed another police raid. The men assumed relaxed positions around the restaurant and only Sonny looked nervous. When the police ars arrived they sauntered in and asked everyone to back up to the wall outside to be searched for illegal weapons. Everyone looked to Tony and he just shrugged so his men moved outside to the wall. Some officers stayed inside with Tony and his three dinner guests and then some strange noises began outside culminating in gunfire.

Tony stood and the police told him to sit. The next surprise was the entry of Sam 'Hitman' Gianetti who had a huge smile on his face.

"Time to go, Tony", he snarled as Tony began to look around for salvation. The fake cops surrounded the four men and led them away.

Sam looked at Sonny before he exited and said, "Love the meatballs!"

Sonny was left with an empty restaurant and a heap of food but was grateful he still had his life.

What happened over the next few weeks was a blur. Sonny and his restaurant became famous for the notoriety of being the scene of the end of the Mafia wars. Sonny cooked his meatballs on every television daytime show that he could go on. His restaurant was full every day and night and they loved his food. He got a television deal with CBC and had his own cook book series entitled 'The Chef to the Mafia' series.

Sonny loved the fame his wholesome food had engendered and began a chain of restaurants all over. The pungent odour of Italian meatballs could now be smelt in every town in the country.

10. Maturity

"I wish you'd just grow up and listen" David James said to his recalcitrant son.

"I am grown up you just don't understand me" his son Brian yelled back.

"If you think you're grown up then act like it" David responded even though he knew they had said the same things before.

"I do!" Brian screamed as he slammed his bedroom door.

"I just can't communicate with that boy" he complained to his wife, Sally. "When will he ever reach some level of maturity?"

She sighed as she too had heard it all before. Her son and husband would never agree on anything and as Brian got older he began to assert himself. She worried about the effect these arguments would have on the other children as Brian got more and more aggressive and rude. They had talked often and hard about how his getting older would make him more mature but it had just increased the conflict. Unlike cheese and wine which got better with maturity Brian just seemed to become more withdrawn.

"I have no idea what to do with him anymore" she said sadly to her husband. "He's not a bad person but he just can't seem to control himself."

"We should have sent him to that boarding school. That would give him some discipline and maturity. He needs a firm hand."

Things never seemed to get better with Brian and the last few months had been hard as he began to stop being the little boy they saw him as and the man he thought he was. This maturity thing was hard on everyone and their seemed no solution that would satisfy everyone. All David and Sally's friends with teenage kids had the same problem. Boys or girls made no difference the problems were similar and they had no solutions either. They were all the same.

"I was never like that, ever', said David. "We had respect for our elders and our teachers. Why have things changed so much?"

The imponderable question hung in the air.

"We just have to be patient, dear" replied Sally. "He will mature one day and we will miss him being a child."

"Maybe" said David, "but I have my doubts. This maturity thing is just too hard!"

12. Challenge

The Challenge was designed to withstand almost everything that space could throw at it. The deflector shields could almost withstand a full blown asteroid collision and it was armed with molecular phasers which would deter most enemy ships. The Challenge was the newest craft in the New Union and was to pave the way to find habitable planets in the Boss Galaxy. With Earth completely covered in buildings and no habitable areas left new places for the increasingly huge population had to be found. Reclamation from the sea had gone slowly and poorly and the decision had been made to go out and establish new colonies like the ones in the Nion Galaxy which had proven successful.

Captain Johannes powered the ship up and spoke to his five man crew. He told them that the trip was exploratory and their work was mainly maintenance because of the organic computer system that controlled almost all components of the ship. This system also tapped into his mind and could be thought controlled. Return was planned for three years and they would have a heroes welcome if they could meet the challenge and discover new habitable worlds. For the Captain this journey would be the pinnacle of his career if he was successful. He had no idea what they would confront but felt the ship could handle it.

Challenge as the ship's computer was called kept them on course through ion drive speed which enabled them to spacejump and make great time out of their own galaxy. None the less it took seven months to reach the Boss Galaxy and begin to plot planets. Sitting in unknown space they managed to find seven planets that looked suitable and sent drones to check on atmosphere. Six returned with positives and the seventh was seemingly lost. Quickly they began to move around the vast distances between the planets to collect samples and details for the first wave of colonisers. Unfortunately for them each planet, while suitable offered nothing more than climate and atmosphere – they found no new or large deposits of valuable minerals, medicinal plants or even advanced life.

Captain Johannes decided to plot a course for the unknown planet the drone failed to return from. It was his last chance to make a name for himself. The planet loomed large in the viewscreen and Challenge seemed hesitant to enter the planet's orbit. He wondered why the spaceship's computer was jittery and asked telepathically. He felt the words 'unknown cause' and felt this must have been a glitch in the programming. Johannes thought about pulling away but he remembered his own words about confronting whatever came his way and continued the entry process.

He felt a scream in his head and it seemed that Challenge was being destroyed. A calm voice then said to him, "Thank you for coming to our planet. We look forward to studying you in the years ahead. Do not try to escape we have control of your ship and will bring you in."

Captain Johannes knew that this was one challenge he wasn't going to conquer.

13. Development

'NO HOUSES HERE' screamed the sign stuck to the telegraph pole. Brian Georges mentally shrugged and kept driving. He had seen all this before in his long years as a developer. People were always afraid of change, afraid of progress and often hated him passionately. This never worried or deterred him; uncertainty was not in his vocabulary. The Nappa Valley would become his newest housing estate and make him a packet. Of course their would be opposition from greenies, hippies and other types like that but his money and contacts would make it happen.

'NO CONCRETE IN THE VALLEY', 'NO TRUCKS', 'WHAT ABOUT THE ENVIRONMENT?' each pole had a hand drawn sign as he drove past to the site. This was just an exploratory trip and to attend the public meeting at the local Progress Association Hall. He new the meeting was a waste of time and he would be abused but the local council liked it on the Development Application and he liked to tick all the boxes. The valley was the perfect site for a huge housing estate and he had picked up most of the land cheap. When some locals found out the howling started. The local paper picked up the story and had ignored his jobs, growth and progress line for a save the whatever and our local agricultural lifestyle.

Arriving in the historic little town of Nappa he parked and went into the busy café where he saw some brochures for tonight's meeting. Casually dressed he didn't want to draw attention to himself and sat down in the corner. He ordered coffee and a salad sandwich and settled back to listen and observe as the customers went about their lunches. He detected some conversation about the meeting and when the crowd slowed and left he asked the waitress what the meeting was about. She said it was about saving the town and she didn't want too many houses either although business would pick-up.

As he left he thought she should get ready for plenty of business as he would have hundreds of workmen here soon. Heading to the little B and B where he was staying Brian thought about his developments and what they did for communities. Popular opinion was always anti-development but people needed houses to live in and shops to buy necessities. He had never understood all the opposition he engendered but admired those who fought for a cause that could only lead to inevitable defeat.

Brian thought to himself that the attempts to constrain development would always be doomed because of human nature. People needed jobs, places to live and the chance to make a dollar. As he dressed for the meeting he thought of all the words that would be wasted, the cost to him to cater for all their concerns and what it added to the cost of construction. He knew the world wouldn't change and that progress was inevitable. He intended to be at the forefront of that change as his business depended on it.

14. Experiment

Dr Frankenstein was a lonely and embittered man. He had lost everything in his quest to create life. The monster he had created had destroyed his family and friends, ruined his career and nearly sent him crazy. It took all his resources to get back to Frankfurt from chasing the monster all the way to the North Pole. While the thing had escaped Dr Frankenstein thought humanity was now safe as his creation had been driven far away from people.

Now back at his home he found himself getting more and more depressed as the hollow rooms echoed at every noise and he missed his family deeply. He spent his days in aimless lethargy not wanting to have anything to do with his old life or career. He hadn't been back to the laboratory where he had made his two greatest creations and two biggest mistakes. Months passed and he became thinner and more insular than he'd ever been. Never one for a social life he was happiest in his books and work. Soon his loneliness and regret began to cling to him like a parasite. It was a feeling he couldn't divest himself of and it began to drive him mad.

Now in the seemingly endless days and nights he began to talk to himself. He discussed scientific methodology and began to analyse out loud what had gone wrong before. Soon he had talked himself into the idea that he could succeed , he could create life and that it would not turn out like his two other projects. In his madness he became clever and tidied himself up before going out in public and reopening his laboratory. He now had the time to create the perfect life and he chose to recreate his dead son – the first murdered innocent.

Much of Dr Frankenstein's materials and equipment were still where he had left them all those years ago. Setting to work in a frenzy he cleaned and brewed and plotted. Of course he needed fresh body parts but this had never been a problem. He watched the streets and read the newspapers for details of deaths and burials. This work was exacting but soon he had garnered enough parts from his grave-digging that he could create his own son again. He was completely absorbed in his madness, he feared nothing, especially consequences.

He had to wait weeks for the right night. Finally the storm he required raged over the city and he connected the wires. Electricity brought life to the inanimate figure prone on the trolley. It twitched and shook as its parts began to feel life again. The small body began to move and sit up looking strangely around. Dr Frankenstein was ecstatic he had done it again and now had the son he had lost. The experiment had worked.

They stared at each other and yet neither saw the madness in the eyes of the other. Perhaps this time it would work out for both of them.

15. Road

The road wound its way around the mountain to the small hamlet of George's Cross. Jamie hadn't been back for years. He had gone away to university after school and then had never found a reason to go back. Now he had to come back to attend his grandmother's funeral and he dreaded seeing his parents again. He had left on bad terms and had never been able to understand their desire for him to continue on with the family business. He hated oyster farming and the long hours for little money. Now he made a good living as an illustrator but they saw this as a stop-gap until he got a real job.

Driving through the little village he began to remember all the little things he liked about the town. The close knit community feel where everyone helped each other and the links between families that stretch back for generations. The river life hardened people but it also made them good people for the most. You could always get credit at the general store and the small school had been a great place to make friends. It was here he'd met Sally McCarthy his first and only real love.

Smiling at the memory from all those years ago he drove along the river road thinking how much he missed the river and how it drew you to it. Reality again sunk in as he turned into the short driveway that led to his parent's house on the river. He could clearly see the ephemera of years of oyster farming, the old boats, the timber frames, the shells and the old wooden jetty that looked as if it could be swept away by a boat's wake. His home looked the same, except a little more worn out and it needed a paint.

Turning the engine off Jamie could hear the heat clicking off the engine as it dissipated. He didn't want to leave the safety and comfort of his car but his mother appeared at the door and rushed to meet him. He quickly got himself together and opened the door to his Volkswagen. She hugged him hard and held him back to get a good look as she welcomed him effusively. He felt slightly embarrassed but was more nervous about seeing his father again. His mother had never been part of the problem that had driven him away.

Then his father appeared as if by magic around the back of the shed near the water. He looked from a distance slightly older, slightly more stooped but still a large and powerful man. As Jamie walked toward him he thought of their last time together and the acrimony it had caused. His father shook him by the hand and welcomed him home. Jamie couldn't think of anything to say and the tension increased. Jamie's father explained how glad they were to see him home again. He hoped Jamie was doin' fine and that it would be a good visit.

Visibly relaxed Jamie now looked at the river and hoped the past could be just that. He was older now and they could begin again. He would never work the river but he could be part of a family again.

16. Adventure

Michael Ducrois desperately needed an idea. His career had floundered badly and he needed to produce this time. He had considered all the genres but had come back to the one he knew best, adventure. He had once produced and directed some of the greatest adventure films ever, the Crosswhite series with that great hero Danny Crosswhite adventurer and raconteur. All Ducrois needed now was a plot that held together a film that consisted of action shot after action shot. Nobody really wanted plot anymore anyway – it was all about the action.

He was excited by this and began to think of a basic storyline. He thought to himself do I need some romance? What about a sidekick? Exotic locations? What stars? Do I need stars or just young actors? Big stunts – filmgoers love stunts and special effects. All these thoughts went through his mind as he drove to his studio office. He needed something by the end of the day as the presentation was tomorrow and it was make or break after his last romantic comedy failed – he'd always hated love.

Sitting down at his desk he fired up the laptop and began to think of all the successful films he and others had done in the past. What worked – the archaeologist thing went well back in the 1980s – time for a revival. Let's set it at an archaeological excavation where they dig up – what? – Something dangerous or mystical - and this leads to more adventure and chases and shootouts. The hero will be the son of Danny Crosswhite and we can bring Danny in to capture the older generation market as well. Ducrois laughed to himself, he considered himself a genius and this was proving it again.

His mind raced as he planned each scene carefully in his head. These films needed very little dialogue as audiences didn't care about the subtleties. Okay he thought this is it; follow the pattern that they love. The hero is made through circumstance, his father returns as a mentor, he has to save the world but runs into life threatening complications, he falls in love –loses her and then gets her back and finally a hint of the next adventure to tease audiences. The studio will love it he thought. Never mind it's been done before a million times. The takings on the first release weekend are the only guide to greatness. Even rubbish gets awards these days if the studio pumps enough money into it.

Ducrois imagined being back on the A-list of celebrities and mixing it on the red carpet with all the stars. The parties, the television shows, the opening night and the power again. Oh how he missed the power of being the best. He could see himself picking and choosing what big budget blockbuster to do next. This film would make Avatar look cheap. This film would be his return, the start of a new adventure for him.